A-Town Crowned

**Atlanta Braves
World Series Champions**

A Story 26 Years in the Making

Book design by **ANDREA ZAGATA** and **JOSH CRUTCHMER**

Book photos by The Associated Press and Getty Images.

Contents

The Atlanta Braves celebrate the 2021 World Series championship after a 7-0 win at Houston, completing a six-game series win.

CHAMPIONS
2021 WORLD SERIES CHAMPS
021 WORLD SERIES CHAMPIONS
ATLANTA BRAVES
CONGRATULATIONS
2021 WORLD SE
D SERIES
2021

On top of the world!

Atlanta Braves. World Champions!

Sounds pretty good doesn't it? Atlanta fans have waited 26 long years to utter those words, and finally, the Braves are back on top.

Let the celebration begin!

In what has to be considered one of the greatest turnarounds in Major League history, the Braves absorbed the loss of superstar Ronald Acuña Jr. and rode the trade deadline moves made by GM Alex Anthopoulos to a dominant second half run. The Braves obtained outfielders Eddie Rosario, Adam Duvall and Jorge Soler along with reliever Richard Rodríguez just hours before the July 30 trade deadline, adding to the acquisition of outfielder Joc Pederson two weeks earlier. With the added firepower the Braves were finally able to climb above.500 for the first time on August 8th. The acquisition of Rosario, Duvall and Pederson paid huge dividends as the three would go on to combine to drive in 17 of Atlanta's 28 runs in its six-game NL Championship Series win over the defending champion Los Angeles Dodgers. Written off by many when veteran pitcher Charlie Morton went down with a broken leg in Game 1, the Braves used timely hitting and clutch pitching on their way to a World Series win over the powerful Houston Astros.

In the following pages we proudly bring you on a trip down memory lane of this championship season that came to its jubilant conclusion in Houston, TX.

A-Town Crowned provides Braves fans the best view in the house of all the ups and downs of the season and gives you an inside look at the incredible World Series win 26 years in the making.

Our heartfelt congratulations go out to Braves GM Alex Anthopoulos, Manager Brian Snitker and his staff, and the entire Braves team on their accomplishments this season. Celebrate this season Atlanta, and save this book to revisit the Braves' magical moments and unforgettable team – both stars and role players – who rewarded your faith with a World Championship.

Congratulations Atlanta Braves! Let's do it again soon.

Housewarming Party

Acuña the standout as the Braves entertain a home crowd for the first time in two seasons.

April 9, 2021

ATLANTA — Ronald Acuña Jr. and the Atlanta Braves put on quite a show for their first home crowd since 2019.

Acuña had four hits, including a long two-run homer that gave Atlanta the lead, and made a leaping catch to support Charlie Morton's six strong innings, leading the Braves to an 8-1 win over the Philadelphia Phillies on Friday night.

Acuña's fifth-inning blast off Zack Wheeler (1-1) traveled an estimated 456 feet, landing deep in the center-field seats behind the Braves bullpen for a 2-1 lead.

"That was probably one of the harder ones I've hit," Acuña said through a translator.

Acuña also had two doubles and showed his speed by beating out an infield single in the eighth.

"That just shows the complete player that he is," Braves manager Brian Snitker said.

Morton (1-1) permitted one run and four hits. The veteran right-hander struck out seven and walked one.

"That was the best my curveball has felt and I felt really good throwing it," Morton said.

Pinch hitter Ehire Adrianza connected for a three-run homer and Freddie Freeman added a two-run shot as Atlanta's hitters shook off a slow start to the season. The Braves were held to a combined three runs while being swept in a three-game series at Philadelphia last week to open the season.

Leading 3-1, Morton escaped the sixth inning with runners on first and third when Acuña made a leaping catch of Alec Bohm's drive at the warning track in right field.

Morton, 37, won his first home start with Atlanta since his 2008 rookie season. He returned to Atlanta as a free agent following 12 seasons with Pittsburgh, Houston and Tampa Bay.

Adrianza was reinstated from the restricted list before the game. His homer off Brandon Kintzler in the sixth drove in Austin Riley and Cristian Pache, who reached on errors by Bohm at third base. Freeman's homer off David Hale in the eighth pushed the lead to 8-1.

Wheeler, who threw 94 pitches, allowed three runs and seven hits in 4 2/3 innings.

Andrew McCutchen's run-scoring single in the third gave Philadelphia a 1-0 lead.

The Braves won their home opener before a crowd of 14,302 as fans returned after being kept away during the pandemic in 2020. The Braves are allowing about one-third of the seats at Truist Park to be used in their first homestand. They plan to expand that to 50% in their next homestand.

Ronald Acuña Jr. watches his home run during the Braves 2021 season home opener against the Phillies on April 09, 2021 at Truist Park.

Fried Provides Fireworks

Pitcher steps up as pinch-hitter to deliver game-winner at Truist Park on Independence Day.

July 4, 2021

ATLANTA — Max Fried never thought he would get the chance for a game-winning hit. After all, Fried is a pitcher.

Thanks to Atlanta's depleted bench, it happened on Sunday. And Fried delivered.

The pinch-hitting pitcher lined a bases-loaded single up the middle in the 10th inning, and the Braves rallied for a wild 8-7 victory over the Miami Marlins.

"It's something you always dream about happening, but when I knew I was going to be a pitcher I figured it would never be reality," Fried said.

Fried isn't a normal pitcher. He is hitting .300 this season. He had 11 hits, including four doubles, while driving in four runs in 2019, when he hit .196.

"If Max wasn't pitching he would be an outfielder in the big leagues," Braves manager Brian Snitker said.

Fried was called on to hit with the Braves out of position players after a four-run rally in the ninth. He singled on a 3-1 pitch off Anthony Bass (1-4), driving in Dansby Swanson from third base and drawing his jubilant teammates out of the dugout.

"That was probably as good as I've felt on the field finishing out a game," Fried said.

Fried's game-ending swing was a big surprise to Marlins manager Don Mattingly, who assumed the pitcher was hoping for a walk.

"I really was surprised that he swung the bat there but he's actually a pretty good hitter," Mattingly said.

With the bases loaded and one out in the 10th, Austin Riley was thrown out at the plate when he tried to score on a bases-loaded wild pitch by Bass. Riley was initially called safe before the umpires reversed the call on a review.

The Braves quickly recovered from that disappointment. Bass loaded the bases with an intentional walk to Kevan Smith before giving up Fried's single.

Miami opened a 7-3 lead with three runs in the ninth. Sandy Leon led off with a drive to right for his second homer. Starling Marte singled with two out and scored on Jesús Aguilar's 13th homer against Shane Greene.

But Marlins closer Yimi García struggled in the bottom half, and the Braves rallied.

Orlando Arcia singled in Dansby Swanson, and Abraham Almonte made it 7-6 with a two-run double. Ronald Acuña Jr. then delivered a tying sacrifice fly.

García was charged with four runs and four hits. He walked three, two intentionally.

"Sometimes you've got those days when you make good pitches and they make good contact, too," Garcia said through a translator.

Will Smith (3-5) pitched the 10th for the win. Acuña also hit a two-run homer off Zach Thompson in the third.

Adam Duvall hit a three-run homer and drove in four runs for Miami, which dropped two of three in the series. Aguilar finished with three hits and two RBI.

Duvall, facing his former Atlanta teammates, took the NL lead with 60 RBI. He also ranks among the NL leaders with 19 homers following his sixth-inning drive off Charlie Morton that gave the Marlins a 4-2 lead.

Duvall just missed another homer in the eighth. His blast to the right-field corner off Chris Martin was initially called a homer by first base umpire John Libka.

After Acuña protested in right, the umpires huddled and called the ball foul. The TV replay confirmed it was foul and the Marlins did not argue the ruling.

Max Fried connects on the game-winning hit against the Miami Marlins during the 10th inning on July 4 in Atlanta.

Max Fried, center, is mobbed after making the winning hit against the Miami Marlins.

Suddenly, All Bets Are Off

Expectations upended after star injures ACL and requires season-ending surgery.

July 10, 2021

MIAMI — Braves star Ronald Acuña Jr. will have season-ending surgery to repair a completely torn ACL in his right knee after he was injured during Atlanta's 5-4 win over the Miami Marlins on Saturday.

An MRI showed the severity of the injury and the Braves made the announcement shortly before midnight that their three-time All-Star will be out until at least next year.

Acuña landed awkwardly on his right leg after jumping on the warning track in right field to try to catch a drive from Jazz Chisholm Jr. in the fifth inning. The 23-year-old slammed into the outfield wall and crumbled on the warning track, immediately grabbing his right knee while Chisholm sprinted out an inside-the-park homer.

Acuña tried to walk off but dropped back to the ground in shallow right field. A trainer tended to him while a cart was retrieved, and concerned teammates gathered quietly around him.

Tears welled in his eyes as he waited. When the cart pulled around to the nearby warning track, he had to be helped over and did not put any weight on his right leg.

Braves manager Brian Snitker said immediately after the game that Acuña was undergoing evaluation and the team didn't expect to have news until Sunday morning.

"He's in a lot of pain, I can tell you that. It's a tough break for the team and for him," he said.

Max Fried gave up three straight hits but settled down to retire the side with two strikeouts after the injury.

"You never like to see one of your teammates come up injured after trying to make a great play," Fried said. "It's obviously very unfortunate, but you have to stay with the task at hand and finish the game."

Chisholm at first thought Acuña was going to make the catch and didn't realize the severity of the injury until after he crossed home plate.

"A guy like that, him getting injured, the baseball world is going to miss him if he's out for a long time," Chisholm said. "Hopefully he gets better."

Acuña was slated to start in the outfield for the NL All-Star team in Tuesday's game. He is hitting .283 with 24 home runs and 52 RBI for the three-time defending NL East champions, who started the day in second place behind the New York Mets.

Freddie Freeman had a two-run homer and an RBI single, while Dansby Swanson and Austin Riley ripped doubles as the first three Braves reached base off All-Star pitcher Trevor Rogers (7-6) in the fourth inning. Atlanta has won three straight over Miami.

Acuña doubled in the fifth and scored on Freeman's shot over the right-field wall.

Max Fried (6-5), who went five innings with five strikeouts while surrendering nine hits, had to compose himself quickly after the injury.

"I was just trying to find my rhythm again; it was huge being able to get those last two strikeouts," Fried said. (The injury) is tough, but you have to get your focus back."

Rogers lasted four innings and gave up three runs, two earned, while striking out four and walking two.

Rogers' own miscue led to an unearned run in the third. After walking Jonathan Lucroy, the lefty threw wildly past first baseman Jesus Aguilar. Lucroy later raced home from second on Freeman's single.

Prior to leaving the game in the fifth with mild intercostal soreness, Adam Duvall continued to be a nemesis to his former team. The Marlins slugger lined a two-out double in the first inning and followed that with a two-run single in the third.

The Marlins loaded the bases with one out after Acuña's injury, but Fried struck out Jon Berti and Jorge Alfaro to maintain Atlanta's two-run advantage. Miami left runners on second and third in the first inning, too.

Atlanta right fielder Ronald Acuña Jr., center, is carried to a medical cart after trying to make a catch on an inside-the-park home run hit by Miami's Jazz Chisholm Jr. during the fifth inning on July 10.

Concerned Braves players gather around Ronald Acuña Jr. after the star was injured against the Marlins on July 10.

Walk-Off to Top of NL East

Albies' Blast
Lifts Braves
over Reds in
the 11th.

August 11, 2021

ATLANTA — Ozzie Albies crushed a three-run homer off Lucas Sims in the bottom of the 11th inning, lifting the Atlanta Braves to an 8-6 victory over the Cincinnati Reds on Wednesday night.

Albies' 19th homer sailed 412 feet into the right-field stands to send Truist Park into a wild celebration. He drove in placement runner Adam Duvall and Joc Pederson, whom Sims (4-2) walked.

"I was thinking when I got to home plate of tying the ball game, so I needed a base hit," Albies said. "Once the (at-bat) got rolling, I got my pitch I was looking for. Hitter's count, and I did what I had to do."

With the win, and Philadelphia's loss to the Los Angeles Dodgers, the Braves moved into a tie for first place in the NL East.

"That's a great feeling especially right now," Albies said. "The Phillies (lost), and we won. This game was important for us. Everything for the team. It's enjoyable when you're winning and you see where you're at and fighting for first place to win the division, so everything counts from now on. There's not a lot of the season left, so you just have to keep rolling."

Kyle Farmer singled in the tiebreaking run in the 11th inning against Edgar Santana (3-0), and Joey Votto hit a pair of two-run homers for the Reds.

Votto sent the game into extra innings by taking closer Will Smith deep in the ninth. He went 4 for 5 and reached safely five times.

"I appreciate it," Cincinnati manager David Bell said of Votto. "I respect it. Like everyone else, it's fun watching it. It's amazing. He's a great hitter. It's really nice watching him go through it. I probably am out of (accolades) to say, but it's something to really appreciate and enjoy as we watch it happen."

The Braves didn't trail until Barnhart's single. Guillermo Heredia hit an early two-run homer off Wade Miley, and Austin Riley doubled in a pair of runs for Atlanta.

Touki Toussaint pitched five-plus innings for the Braves. He allowed four hits and two runs with three walks and five strikeouts.

Atlanta has won seven of eight. Cincinnati, eight games behind Milwaukee in the NL Central, has lost three straight after winning five in a row.

The Braves led 1-0 in the first. Albies, who was 2 for 18, singled and advanced to second on a walk to Jorge Soler. Albies scored on Riley's double, but Soler ran through third base coach Ron Washington's stop sign and was thrown out at the plate.

Heredia followed with his fifth homer in the second to make it 3-0. Atlanta struck again in the third when Freddie Freeman singled and scored from first on Riley's double down the left-field line. Riley scored for a 5-0 lead on Dansby Swanson's sacrifice fly.

Freeman was ruled safe after a video review overturned the call that he was originally tagged out.

Smith blew his fourth save of the season when Votto homered.

Toussaint was cruising until the sixth. He hit Nick Castellanos with a pitch before Votto took him deep to center with his 24th homer, trimming the lead to 5-2. Jesse Chavez, Toussaint's replacement, struck out Barnhart and pinch-hitter Jonathan India to strand two runners.

Miley gave up five runs and five hits with three walks and four strikeouts. In his previous 13 starts since May 14, Miley had gone 5-1 with a 2.30 ERA.

"We battled back," Miley said. "The offense did a great job. Joey had an outstanding day. It's tough to lose a game like that. We fought our way back in it, took the lead in the 11th, but tip your cap. Ozzie got a pitch and put a good swing on it."

Atlanta second baseman Ozzie Albies hits a walk-off three-run home run in the bottom of the 11th inning against Cincinnati to send the Braves into a tie atop the National League East.

The Braves' Jorge Soler and Cincinnati catcher Tucker Barnhart end up face-to-face on a play at home plate on August 11.

Braves Clinch Division Title

NL East crown comes to Atlanta again, but this time the title might be a bit more satisfying.

September 30, 2021

ATLANTA — The Atlanta Braves have done it all before — many, many times before — but this one felt a bit different.

More satisfying, for sure.

After all, the Braves floundered under .500 much of the season. They endured devastating injuries and grim legal issues. They had to essentially rebuild their outfield at the trade deadline.

And yet there they were Thursday night, swigging champagne, puffing on cigars and celebrating an NL East championship.

Ian Anderson turned in another dominant pitching performance, Jorge Soler and Austin Riley homered to power the offense, and the Braves clinched their fourth straight division title by completing a sweep of the Philadelphia Phillies with a 5-3 victory.

"We were just trying to hang in there and pull this thing off," manager Brian Snitker said. "It's unbelievable what these guys accomplished with everything we went through."

The Braves didn't climb above .500 until Aug. 6, yet they went on to capture their 21st division title — more than any other team — since moving from Milwaukee to Atlanta in 1966.

They'll face their former city in the playoffs when they open the best-of-five Division Series at the NL Central champion Brewers on Oct. 8.

"It's a great feeling," first baseman Freddie Freeman said. "We had a lot of ups and down, so many things that could have derailed us."

Atlanta's very first hitter got things rolling in the division-clinching triumph. Soler hit the first leadoff homer of his career, going deep for the 26th time this season on a 3-2 pitch from Kyle Gibson (4-6).

Riley, bolstering his improbable MVP candidacy, added to the lead with his 33rd homer in the fourth. He drove in another run with a broken-bat single in the fifth to extend the lead to 5-0.

Ozzie Albies, who also figures to be part of the MVP race, threw his support to Riley.

"He's been carrying this team," Albies said. "He did a great, great job. He had a great season."

It was more than enough run support for Anderson (9-5), who appears to be rounding into the sort of form he showed during the 2020 postseason as a rookie.

Anderson pitched six innings of one-hit ball before yielding a two-run homer to Andrew McCutchen in the seventh. A.J. Minter, Luke Jackson and Will Smith worked the final three innings, with Smith breezing through the ninths to earn his 37th save.

In a way, the finish was a bit out of character considering all the obstacles that were thrown Atlanta's way.

Star outfielder Ronald Acuña Jr. was lost to a season-ending knee injury, while former ace Mike Soroka didn't make an expected comeback after tearing his Achilles tendon for the second time.

In addition, slugging outfielder Marcell Ozuna — the pot-stirring leader of the Braves' run to Game 7 of last year's NL Championship Series — was arrested after an altercation with his wife in late May and didn't return to the team.

General manger Alex Anthopoulos pulled off a flurry of moves at the trade deadline, assembling an entirely new outfield that included Soler, Adam Duvall and Eddie Rosario.

The Braves spent 126 days without a winning record — the most by a division champ since the 1989 Toronto Blue Jays and fourth-most since the divisional era began in 1969, according to Elias Sports.

The Braves gained sole possession of the NL East lead for the first time Aug. 15 while in the midst of a perfect 9-0 road trip and never relinquished the top spot.

When Smith struck out Ronald Torreyes for the final out, it was time for another Atlanta celebration before a near-sellout crowd of 38,235.

Atlanta second baseman Ozzie Albies launches an RBI double in the fifth inning of a 5-3 win over the Phillies on September 30.

Jorge Soler follows through on a solo home run in the bottom of the first inning in a division-clinching win over the Phillies.

The Braves celebrate the NL East title in a fountain at Truist Park after a win over the Phillies.

Patient Brewers Hang On

Tellez homer, throw spark Brewers in Game 1.

Brewers 2
Braves 1

Brewers lead series, 1-0

October 8, 2021

MILWAUKEE — Rowdy Tellez fouled off Charlie Morton's pitch in a scoreless game, then headed toward the dugout for a deep breath and a new bat.

Just the break the Milwaukee Brewers needed.

Tellez spoiled Morton's gem by hitting a two-run homer in the seventh inning, leading the Brewers over the Atlanta Braves 2-1 in the opener of their NL Division Series.

"I'm still out of breath," Tellez said. "It was a crazy moment."

Corbin Burnes, Adrian Houser and Josh Hader combined on a four-hitter that gave Milwaukee the early lead in this best-of-five series.

Former Brewer Orlando Arcia grounded to second with runners on the corners to end the game. That came after Milwaukee catcher Omar Narváez — who combined with first baseman Tellez on a key first-inning double play — blocked Hader's 1-2 pitch in the dirt to keep Freddie Freeman at third base.

Neither team produced much offense until the Brewers finally broke through in the seventh.

After Morton (0-1) plunked Avisaíl García with a 1-2 pitch to start the inning, Tellez ripped another 1-2 offering from Morton over the center-field wall to break a scoreless tie.

"Even in those at-bats, I got them where I wanted to be," Morton said. "I just didn't finish them off. I hit Avi, and then I grooved one to Rowdy."

Tellez was 1 for 13 against the Braves this season until delivering that 411-foot drive, which came immediately after the hefty, bearded slugger fouled a pitch off.

"I don't know if I broke that bat," Tellez said. "I just saw something fly off of it. I was like, 'I need all the help I can get right now.'

"I walked back, and the bat boy didn't even realize. I kind of just collected my breath and calmed myself, got back to the box, and I said, '(Keep) my foot down and just see the pitch and hit the ball hard.' That's all I wanted to do."

The big hit capped quite a comeback for Tellez, who was activated from the injured list Saturday after missing about three weeks with a right patella strain.

"It was a tight timetable," Brewers manager Craig Counsell said. "We knew it was going to be tight. We were fortunate that he got himself healthy. The training staff did a heck of a job."

Atlanta's Joc Pederson lofted a pinch-hit homer off Houser (1-0) with two outs in the eighth.

Morton's 85th and final pitch to Tellez was among the few mistakes he made all day. He struck out nine, walked one and hit a batter to continue his recent history of exceptional postseason performances.

Burnes was every bit as good in his first career postseason start.

The NL Cy Young Award contender opened the game with two straight walks and threw 40 pitches in the first two innings but settled down from there. The right-hander struck out six and gave up two hits and three walks in six shutout innings, throwing 91 pitches.

"They're an aggressive offense," Burnes said. "That was kind of the key tonight was to try to play off of that. We were just trying to do too much early on."

After the Braves put runners on the corners with nobody out but failed to score in the top of the first, nobody got a runner past first base until Tellez homered.

Atlanta's best scoring chance came at the start of the game.

Burnes walked the first two batters he faced — Jorge Soler and Freeman — with Soler advancing to third on a passed ball.

Ozzie Albies followed with a sharp grounder down the first-base line that Tellez caught just before stepping on the bag. When he noticed Soler was trying to score from third, Tellez threw to the plate.

Narváez caught the one-hop throw and tagged Soler to complete the double play.

Atlanta's Jorge Soler is tagged out at home by Milwaukee catcher Omar Narvaez during Game 1.

Emphatically, All Square

Fried sharp, Braves blank
Brewers 3-0 to tie NLDS

Braves 3, Brewers 0

Series tied, 1-1

October 9, 2021

MILWAUKEE — Max Fried says his strategy in pressure situations is to avoid making too much of the moment.

The approach that worked so well for the Atlanta Braves left-hander in the regular season also is paying dividends in the playoffs.

Fried pitched six sharp innings and Atlanta's bullpen held on after manager Brian Snitker's quick hook, sending the Braves over the Milwaukee Brewers 3-0 to tie their NL Division Series at a game apiece.

"He was phenomenal — all you could ask for," said Atlanta's Austin Riley, who homered in the sixth inning. "He came out, pounded the zone. He's been doing that since the All-Star break."

Once Fried was pulled, it got more dicey for the Braves.

The Brewers brought the tying run to the plate against Atlanta's bullpen in each of the last three innings but couldn't get a key hit. They couldn't do much of anything against Fried, who has allowed just one earned run over 29 innings in his last four starts.

Fried struck out nine, gave up three hits and didn't walk anybody. The Brewers didn't get a runner in scoring position until Willy Adames hit a two-out double in the sixth, and Fried responded by striking out Eduardo Escobar.

"He's just a really good pitcher, executing a lot of pitches," Brewers manager Craig Counsell said. "It spells a tough night for the offense."

Fried went 7-0 with a 1.46 ERA over his last 11 regular-season starts while pitching his best down the stretch.

Braves starting pitcher Max Fried throws against the Brewers during the first inning of Game 2 of the NLDS in Milwaukee.

Fried delivered again Saturday as the Braves bounced back from a 2-1 loss in Game 1.

"You just try to focus and realize that this is the same game we've been playing all year," Fried said. "The stakes might be a little bit higher, but you go out there and make the pitch that you're supposed to make, that's going to trump all."

This was the second straight exceptional outing by a Braves starter in a series that has been dominated by pitching.

Atlanta's Charlie Morton held Milwaukee scoreless through six innings in Game 1, but allowed a two-run homer to Rowdy Tellez in the seventh inning on his 85th and final pitch.

Snitker made sure Fried didn't get that far. Fried had thrown 81 pitches when he was pulled for a pinch-hitter in the top of the seventh.

"He bled it out there in the sixth," Snitker said. "He went through the meat of their lineup and expended what I felt was a lot of energy right there, in a real big moment in playoff baseball. Charlie's been through this 100 times. Max is just cutting his teeth with all this."

The move nearly gave Atlanta two extra runs. After pinch-hitter Joc Pederson singled, Jorge Soler hit a deep drive that left fielder Christian Yelich caught in front of the wall.

Then the Brewers made things interesting against Atlanta's bullpen.

After Luke Jackson struck out the first two batters he faced in the seventh, Luis Urías singled and Lorenzo Cain walked. Tyler Matzek replaced Jackson and got out of the jam by striking out pinch-hitter Tyrone Taylor.

"I thought in those three innings, we got runners on base," Counsell said. "We had some pitches to hit. And we just fouled them off."

The Braves pulled ahead for good with two runs in the third off Brandon Woodruff.

The Braves' Austin Riley celebrates a home run against Milwaukee Brewers the sixth inning of Game 2 of the NLDS.

Atlanta's Freddie Freeman scores past Milwaukee Brewers catcher Manny Pina during the third inning.

Series Turns on One Swing

Pederson smacks a three-run homer, Braves cruise.

Braves 3
Brewers 0

Braves lead series, 2-1

October 11, 2021

ATLANTA — Joc Pederson kept enhancing his "Joctober" nickname with a three-run, pinch-hit homer and the Atlanta Braves shut down Milwaukee once again, beating the Brewers 3-0 to take a 2-1 edge in the NL Division Series.

In a matchup dominated by pitching, Ian Anderson and the Braves bullpen combined on a five-hitter and won by a 3-0 score for the second straight game.

Boosted by shortstop Dansby Swanson's athletic defense, Atlanta can try to reach its second straight NL Championship Series when it hosts Game 4 on Tuesday.

Pederson's homer in the fifth inning was his second of the series. Each drive came as a pinch-hitter against Adrian Houser. Pederson singled as a pinch-hitter in his only other at-bat in this series, and has driven in four of Atlanta's seven runs.

Pederson has hit 11 postseason home runs overall and helped the Los Angeles Dodgers win the World Series last year with his longballs. He then signed as a free agent with the Chicago Cubs in the winter and was traded to Atlanta in July.

"I think the sample size is big enough, right, that that's just who he is," Swanson said of Pederson. "He was in an organization before coming here that obviously had high expectations, just like we do. And he was thrown into pressure situations the last five or six years.

"And, it's important to have those guys on your team come this time of year that you can throw them into any situation and you expect them to be able to produce. And he just comes up with big at-bat after big at-bat. Like Ian (Anderson) said, I'm glad he's on our team."

How does Pederson do it? How does he step up in so many situations when others seem to wilt?

"Treat all the moments the same," Pederson said. "And then not making any moments bigger than what they need to be. And that's kind of just how I look at it. And I just feel like I do the same that I do during the year. But I don't know, there's no secret recipe. I wish there was."

Since winning the opening game of the series, the NL Central champion Brewers have not scored in 19 consecutive innings. They were 0 for 8 with runners in scoring position.

Anderson was dominant for the NL East champion Braves, allowing three hits over five innings with no walks and six strikeouts. Will Smith, the fourth Braves reliever, pitched a perfect ninth for his second save of the series.

Milwaukee starter Freddy Peralta pitched four scoreless innings and was pulled for a pinch-hitter when the Brewers threatened in the fifth.

Houser gave up singles to Travis d'Arnaud and Swanson to open the fifth. Pederson, hitting for Anderson, pulled a high fastball deep into the right-field seats for a 3-0 lead.

Adam Duvall made a crucial baserunning mistake when he tried to advance from first to second as Austin Riley tried to score from third on d'Arnaud's flyball in the second. Left fielder Christian Yelich nailed Duvall for the third out before Riley crossed the plate, costing Atlanta a run.

Milwaukee center fielder Lorenzo Cain, running at full speed, crashed into the wire fence as he tried to catch Duvall's drive in the fourth. Cain held the ball in his glove before hitting the ground and losing control. Cain stayed down as Duvall raced to third with the two-out triple.

Cain remained in the game after a visit from manager Craig Counsell and a trainer. Peralta struck out Eddie Rosario to end the inning.

The Brewers couldn't score in the fifth after putting runners on second and third with no outs. Urías, hit by a pitch, moved to third on a double by Omar Narváez.

Anderson escaped when Cain's sharp grounder was stopped by a diving Swanson, who held the baserunners before throwing to first. Urías was caught in a rundown on pinch-hitter Daniel Vogelbach's grounder to third base, and Kolten Wong lined out to Freddie Freeman at first base to end the inning.

Atlanta shortstop Dansby Swanson turns a double play as Milwaukee shortstop Willy Adames looks back during Game 3 of the NLDS at Truist Park.

The Braves celebrate the three-run home run by Joc Pederson that decided Game 3 of the NLDS.

The American flag stretches across the outfield during pre-game ceremonies ahead of Game 3.

Freeman for Victory

Braves roll into NLCS after dramatic eighth-inning home run to finish Brewers.

Braves 5
Brewers 4

Braves win series, 3-1

October 12, 2021

ATLANTA — Freddie Freeman and the Atlanta Braves will get another chance to finish the job they came agonizingly close to achieving a year ago.

It doesn't matter at all that they had fewer wins than any other playoff team.

Freeman hit an improbable, tiebreaking homer off Milwaukee closer Josh Hader with two outs in the eighth inning and the Braves advanced to the NL Championship Series for the second year in a row, finishing off the Brewers 5-4.

The Braves won the best-of-five Division Series three games to one, advancing to face either the 107-win San Francisco Giants or the 106-win Los Angeles Dodgers with a trip to the World Series on the line.

"I've had a lot of cool moments in my career," Freeman said. 'I think that's gonna top 'em all. Hopefully it's not the last one and I've got a couple more in these playoffs."

The game was tied at 4 when the Brewers brought on Hader to make sure it stayed that way. The hard-throwing lefty struck out Eddie Rosario and Dansby Swanson, but he couldn't get past the 2020 NL MVP.

Freeman caught up with an 84-mph slider, launching a 428-foot drive into the seats in left-center — only the fourth homer all season off Hader, and first since July 28.

Freeman became the first left-hander to homer off Hader since Jason Heyward in 2020.

"The first two guys went down, so I just tried to get a pitch up and he hung a slider and I put a good swing on it," Freeman said. "There was no rhyme or reason to it."

Freeman celebrated wildly on his way around the bases, and popped back out of the dugout for a curtain call as the crowd of 40,195 roared. He became the first player in franchise history to hit a go-ahead home run in the eighth inning or later in a series-clinching win, ESPN Stats & Info said.

"When Freddie hit that ball, I mean, I lost my poise. Everybody in the dugout was going crazy," teammate Ozzie Albies said.

Will Smith pitched a scoreless ninth for his third straight save in the series, getting Christian Yelich to look at strike three with a runner on first for the final out. Tyler Matzek claimed the win with a perfect eighth.

"Freddie! Freddie! Freddie!" the crowd chanted as the Braves celebrated in the center of the field.

Despite having fewer wins (88) than any other playoff team — and even two teams that didn't make the postseason — the NL East champion Braves are headed back to the NLCS for the second season in a row.

A year ago, manager Brian Snitker's team had a 3-1 series lead, only to lose three straight games to the eventual World Series champion Dodgers.

But this team, which floundered under .500 until Aug. 6, overcame so much adversity to clinch its fourth straight division title in the final week.

A season-ending injury to star Ronald Acuña Jr. and legal issues that sidelined Marcell Ozuna forced the Braves to acquire a whole new outfield before the trade deadline.

It paid off.

"We've been feeling really good about ourselves in the second half, playing really good baseball," Freeman said. "We carried it over to the postseason."

Freddie Freeman gets a hug from Will Smith after the Braves clinch the NLDS with a 5-4 win over the Brewers.

Freddie Freeman gets a five from coach Ron Washington after his NLDS-clinching home run.

Eddie Rosario celebrates his two RBI single during the fourth inning.

More Drama, Another W

Riley's game-winning single in 9th lifts Braves past Dodgers.

Braves 3
Dodgers 2

Braves lead series, 1-0

October 16, 2021

ATLANTA — A couple of clutch swings from breakout slugger Austin Riley got the underdog Atlanta Braves off to a fast start in the NL Championship Series. Riley homered and drove in the winning run with a single in the bottom of the ninth inning to give Atlanta a 3-2 victory over the Los Angeles Dodgers in Game 1.

Blake Treinen struck out Freddie Freeman to open the ninth before giving up Ozzie Albies' bloop single to center field. Albies stole second and Riley followed with his line drive into the left-field corner.

"That was my mindset — put something in play and see what happens," Riley said after delivering the first walk-off hit of his career.

The 24-year-old slugger spread his arms in celebration as he rounded first base before getting mobbed by teammates in a happy swarm that carried into shallow center field.

"You dream of that as a little kid," Riley said.

Albies told first-base coach Eric Young Sr. he would be taking off to steal second so he could get in scoring position.

"I knew (Riley) was going to do the job," Albies said.

"As soon as he hit it, I took off. I started yelling, screaming all the way to home plate."

Riley also homered in the fourth. The third baseman set career highs across the board for NL East champion Atlanta this year in his third major league season, batting .303 with 33 homers, 107 RBIs and an .898 OPS in a league-leading 160 games.

"He's come a long way in a short time, I feel like. Even last year, I think that he didn't have all these tools. He can beat you in so many ways now, and he always had that power, but now he's putting together such good at-bats," Dodgers infielder Trea Turner said.

"He's a polished hitter and hats off to him because I think he's gotten to the point where he's been a really good player and there's a reason why fans are chanting MVP for him."

Riley's big game was especially important as Braves first baseman Freddie Freeman struck out four times against four different Los Angeles pitchers after having only one four-strikeout game in the regular season.

Atlanta manager Brian Snitker said Riley has proven he can take that lead role.

"I think that kid has definitely taken the next step forward," Snitker said.

The teams are meeting in the NL Championship Series for the second consecutive season. The Dodgers rallied from a 3-1 deficit to win last year's playoff in seven games before also winning the World Series.

The wild-card Dodgers wasted a scoring opportunity in the top of the ninth. Will Smith got two outs before walking Chris Taylor. Pinch-hitter Cody Bellinger hit a soft single to right field, but Taylor got caught and tagged out in a rundown between second and third that started with right fielder Joc Pederson's throw to shortstop Dansby Swanson.

"I thought if he would have kept going, he might have had a chance at third," Riley said. "But that was a great play by Dansby. Just being able to get out of that inning there was huge."

Corey Knebel worked one inning as the Dodgers' opener in a bullpen game, giving up one run. Eddie Rosario led off with a single, stole second, moved to third on Albies' groundout and scored on Knebel's wild pitch to Riley.

The Dodgers, who won 18 more games than Atlanta during the regular season, pulled even in the second on AJ Pollock's two-out double and Taylor's RBI single.

Will Smith's homer in the fourth, his third of the postseason, gave the Dodgers a 2-1 lead. Riley's two-out homer off Tony Gonsolin in the fourth tied it.

The Dodgers outhit the Braves 10-6 but left runners on base in each of the first seven innings except the fourth. Los Angeles hitters were 1 for 8 with runners in scoring position.

"We prevented runs all night. So we didn't not win the game because we didn't prevent runs," Dodgers manager Dave Roberts said. "We just didn't get the hits when we needed."

Austin Riley, center, is congratulated by teammates after hitting the game winning RBI single to score the Braves' Ozzie Albies in the ninth inning of Game 1 of the NLCS.

Dodgers pitcher Corey Knebel runs to home plate as Atlanta's Eddie Rosario scores on a wild pitch during the first inning of Game 1.

Another Perfect Night

Rosario
delivers
second-
straight walk-
off victory.

Braves 5
Dodgers 4

Braves lead
series, 2-0

October 17, 2021

ATLANTA — More late-night magic has the Atlanta Braves just two wins away from the World Series.

Eddie Rosario delivered Atlanta's second straight walk-off hit in the ninth inning, giving the Braves a 5-4 victory over the Los Angeles Dodgers and a commanding 2-0 lead in the NL Championship Series.

Rosario's fourth hit of the game was a two-out single off shortstop Corey Seager's glove after the Braves twice rallied from two-run deficits.

"These guys have always been like that," Atlanta manager Brian Snitker said. "They're never out."

Rosario delivered a 105-mph scorcher up the middle on the first pitch after closer Kenley Jansen relieved. Seager tried for a backhand snag, but the ball skidded off his glove into center field.

There was no chance to get Dansby Swanson, who raced around from second with the winning run, dropping his helmet as he crossed the plate — a virtual repeat of Game 1 when Austin Riley came through with a winning hit in the ninth for a 3-2 victory.

"We all have that dream, that desire to get to the World Series," Rosario said. "That's just what we're going for."

The Braves are halfway to their first World Series appearance since 1999, but they can't celebrate just yet.

A year ago, Atlanta held leads of 2-0 and 3-1 over the Dodgers in the NLCS, only to lose the last three games of a series played in Arlington, Texas, because the pandemic. Los Angeles went on to beat Tampa Bay in the World Series, while the Braves stewed for another shot.

They rallied in the eighth off Julio Urías, who pitched three hitless innings to finish Game 7 against the Braves last October.

Seventy-three of 87 teams taking 2-0 leads in best-of-seven baseball postseason series have gone on to win.

"We were up on them 2-0 last year, so it's like one of those things where you can't stop now, you got to continue to apply the pressure and come out every day and get after it," Riley said.

Seager and Atlanta's Joc Pederson traded two-run homers — Pederson adding to his "Joctober" lore with his third homer of this postseason and first off his longtime team — before Chris Taylor put the Dodgers ahead again with a two-run, bases-loaded hit in the seventh.

But it was another night of wasted chances for Los Angeles, which went 1 for 10 with runners in scoring position and dropped to 2 for 18 in the series.

Six outs from tying the series, the Dodgers brought in expected Game 4 starter Urías to protect the lead before turning it over to Brusdar Graterol in the ninth.

Rosario led off with a single and tagged up to move up to second on Freddie Freeman's flyout.

Ozzie Albies lined to right for another hit off Urias. Rosario zipped around third as third base coach Ron Washington sent him home, just beating the throw with a brilliant slide that avoided catcher Will Smith's swipe.

Travis d'Arnaud led off the ninth with a broken-bat single to center on a 101 mph pitch from Graterol and was replaced by pinch-runner Cristian Pache. Swanson tried to move Pache along with a bunt, only to have the attempted sacrifice result in a forceout at second when Seager made a backhand stop on Graterol's bounced, offline throw.

Swanson managed to get to second himself when Guillermo Heredia grounded out to third base. The Dodgers turned to their closer to face Rosario, who connected on the very first pitch for the fifth walk-off in 23 postseason games this year.

Braves closer Will Smith ended up with the win after a 1-2-3 ninth.

Eddie Rosario of the
Braves reacts after
hitting a walk-off
single in the ninth
inning of Game 2
against the Dodgers
at Truist Park.

Dodgers catcher Will Smith cannot make the tag on Atlanta Braves Ozzie Albies after a single by Austin Riley in the eighth inning.

Series Gets Interesting

Bellinger, Betts rally Dodgers, cut Atlanta edge in half.

Dodgers 6
Braves 5

Braves lead
series, 2-1

October 19, 2021

LOS ANGELES — Cody Bellinger keeps erasing a forgettable regular season, with his latest big swing putting the Los Angeles Dodgers right back in the NL Championship Series.

Bellinger hit a tying, three-run homer and Mookie Betts then lined an RBI double in the Dodgers' eighth-inning rally, storming back to beat Atlanta 6-5 and cutting the Braves' lead in the series to 2-1.

"It's hard to remember a bigger hit, with what was at stake," Dodgers manager Dave Roberts said. "I'm kind of exhausted now."

Some of the 51,307 fans had already left when the Dodgers were down to their final five outs and facing the daunting prospect of a 3-0 deficit in the series. Bellinger swung and missed two pitches down the middle for strikes, going to his knees in the dirt.

"Ball's coming in hard, some shadows you're dealing with, so I saw it well and I just tried to barrel it up," Bellinger said. "Just continue to barrel up the ball and pass the baton."

Bellinger drove a shoulder-high, 95.6-mph fastball from Luke Jackson into the right-field pavilion, igniting the blue towel-waving crowd and reviving the hopes of the defending World Series champions.

"Sad thing is I would do the same thing again," Jackson said. "I was trying to throw a fastball up and away. I actually threw it better than I thought I threw it. Out of my hand, I was like, `Oh, that's a ball. It's too high.Đ And no, it wasn't too high. Good player, put a good swing on it and pretty remarkable."

Chris Taylor singled, stole second and moved to third on pinch-hitter Matt Beaty's groundout. Betts followed with the double off Jesse Chavez to right-center.

"We can do it, we're confident," Braves manager Brian Snitker said. "There is going to be no residual effects after this game."

The Dodgers had lost all 83 previous postseason games — in both Los Angeles and Brooklyn — in which they trailed by three or more runs in the eighth inning or later.

But that's history now. And so are Bellinger's recent struggles.

"Fresh start," Bellinger said of the postseason. "At least for me this year it's a fresh start. You know, a tough regular season but you know, I felt good towards the end of the season, and just try to continue that feel all the way through."

With the cheering, chanting crowd on its feet in the ninth, Kenley Jansen struck out the side to earn the save, the ninth pitcher used by the Dodgers. They ran through a combined 15 in the first two games.

Staggered with back-to-back walk-off losses in Atlanta, the Dodgers returned home, where they've dominated the Braves in recent years and were an MLB-best 58-23 during the regular season.

The Braves haven't won at Dodger Stadium since June 8, 2018. Going back to the 2013 NLDS, the Braves have dropped 20 of their last 23 in LA — they've lost 10 straight in Los Angeles overall.

It sure looked like they'd end that skid after leading 5-2 in the fifth.

After Corey Seager's two-run shot gave them an early lead, the Dodgers' offense stalled out from the second to eighth innings, with only five hits.

The Braves built their lead with a bunch of singles, pounding out 12 hits, and a dropped flyball by novice center fielder Gavin Lux.

Freddie Freeman broke out of his slump, going 3 for 4 with a walk and a run scored after he struck out seven times in eight at-bats in the first two games.

Adam Duvall went 2 for 5, driving in two runs and scoring another for the Braves. Every Atlanta batter got on base at least once.

Braves pitcher Luke Jackson reacts after giving up a three-run home run to the Dodgers' Cody Bellinger during the eighth inning in Game 3 of the NLCS at Dodger Stadium.

Braves Blast Dodgers

Atlanta goes up 3-1 on Los Angeles for second-straight NLCS.

Braves 9
Dodgers 2

Braves lead series, 3-1

October 20, 2021

LOS ANGELES — Behind the red-hot bat of Eddie Rosario, the Atlanta Braves are one win away from their first World Series appearance since 1999.

All they need to do is put away the defending champion Los Angeles Dodgers. Easier said than done.

After all, the Braves were in exactly the same position last year and failed to finish the job.

Rosario homered twice in his second four-hit game of the NL Championship Series and six Atlanta pitchers combined on a four-hitter, giving the Braves a 9-2 victory for a commanding 3-1 lead in the best-of-seven playoff.

Game 5 is Thursday in Los Angeles. Last year, the Dodgers also trailed 0-2 and 1-3 against Atlanta in the NLCS before roaring back to win three straight games at a neutral site in Arlington, Texas.

"As we saw last year, winning a game is hard, especially a veteran team like this that we're playing," Braves manager Brian Snitker said. "But I feel good about our club just from what we experienced last year and where these guys are."

Adam Duvall and Freddie Freeman also homered for the Braves, who bounced right back from blowing a late lead in an agonizing loss Tuesday to end their 10-game skid at Dodger Stadium.

"I feel like everyone has really hunkered down and dug their heels in and everyone is really focused," Rosario said through a translator. "That's something that I'm really proud to be a part of."

Rosario became the first player to have two four-hit games in a League Championship Series. He drove in four runs and scored three while continuing his torrid postseason hitting, finishing a double short of the cycle. He homered in the second inning, tripled in the third, singled in the fifth and clocked a three-run homer in the ninth.

"As soon as I hit that first home run I just thought to myself, 'Wow, I feel amazing right now,'" Rosario said, "so I kind of just carried that confidence into my other at-bats going forward."

Rosario hit for the cycle last month against San Francisco, achieving the feat on just five total pitches.

"I've been using that bat that I hit for the cycle with and it has not disappointed. I had that double remaining and I'm like, 'Man, this bat has not let me down yet,'" he said. "As soon as I hit that second one out, I go, 'Oh well, there goes the double.'"

The Dodgers will need to jump-start their offense to have a shot at another NLCS comeback. Their first five hitters — Mookie Betts, Corey Seager, NL batting champion Trea Turner, Will Smith and Gavin Lux — were a combined 0 for 17 in Game 4.

Los Angeles, which had won 18 of 19 at home going back to the regular season, has won six consecutive postseason elimination games dating to last year.

"I feel good about it," manager Dave Roberts said. "We have a very resilient team, a very tough team, and it's not going to get much tougher than facing Max Fried in an elimination game, but we've done it before."

Rosario was acquired from Cleveland on July 30 as the Braves remade their depleted outfield before the trade deadline.

What a find he's been.

The left fielder has hit safely in every game this postseason, piling up 14 hits in 30 at-bats (.467) — including a walk-off single in Game 2 against the Dodgers.

Rosario is 10 for 17 (.588) with two homers and six RBIs in the NLCS.

"He's been looking so good at the plate, hitting balls hard," Freeman said.

Atlanta's four homers tied a postseason franchise record.

Each of the series' first three games was decided by one run in the last two innings. But when it got late this time, the wild-card Dodgers couldn't generate any comeback magic.

Freddie Freeman of the Braves hits a solo home run in the third inning of Game 4 of the NLCS against the Dodgers.

Eddie Rosario, right, is congratulated by Freddie Freeman after hitting a two-run home run in the ninth inning of Game 4.

Eddie Rosario slides past Dodgers third baseman Justin Turner on triple during the third inning.

Uneasy, but Still Ahead

Dodgers' rout spurs memories of lost 3-1 lead in 2020 NLCS.

Dodgers 11
Braves 2

Braves lead series, 3-2

October 21, 2021

LOS ANGELES — For a guy who dislikes drama, Chris Taylor sure provided plenty of it.

Taylor hit three homers and drove in six runs, joining the likes of Reggie Jackson and Babe Ruth in October baseball lore, as the Los Angeles Dodgers broke loose at the plate to beat Atlanta 11-2 cutting the Braves' lead to 3-2 in the best-of-seven NL Championship Series.

"It's cool. It's definitely a surreal feeling for me," Taylor said. "I never thought I was going to hit three homers in a game, let alone a postseason game, and it just still hasn't really sunk in."

AJ Pollock had two home runs and four RBIs for the defending champion Dodgers, who have won seven straight postseason elimination games dating to last season. They also trailed 0-2 and 1-3 against Atlanta in the NLCS last year before rallying to win three straight at a neutral site in Texas.

"We needed to make a statement," the mild-mannered Taylor said. "They put it on us yesterday. We had to respond."

Game 6 is Saturday in Atlanta, where the Braves get two more chances to clinch their first trip to the World Series since 1999.

"I guess when our backs are against the wall we play our best and fight, but that's just not an ideal spot to be in," Dodgers manager Dave Roberts said.

After mustering only four hits during a 9-2 loss in Game 4 that pushed them to the brink of elimination, the desperate Dodgers rapped out eight hits by the third inning off Max Fried. They finished with 17, a club record for a postseason game, and also equaled a postseason franchise mark with five home runs.

The Dodgers got to Fried with four consecutive hits in the second. Pollock hit a tying homer and Taylor drove the first pitch he saw to left field, putting Los Angeles in front for good, 3-2.

Starting in place of injured Justin Turner at third base, Taylor became the second Dodgers player with a three-homer game in the playoffs. Kiké Hernández also did it in Game 5 of the 2017 NLCS against the Chicago Cubs at Wrigley Field as Los Angeles won its first pennant in 29 years.

Taylor had an RBI single in the third to make it 4-2. He went deep in the fifth, sending an 0-2 pitch from Chris Martin to center field and extending the lead to 6-2.

Taylor homered again in the seventh, taking Dylan Lee out to left-center before taking a curtain call in the dugout.

"He's just super calm and he's so consistent for us," Pollock said. "Maybe the three home runs might have spiked his adrenaline, but probably not."

Los Angeles got a clutch performance from its bullpen, too, after opener Joe Kelly allowed a two-run homer to Freddie Freeman in the first and soon exited after 28 pitches with tightness in his right biceps that will sideline him for the rest of the postseason.

Evan Phillips, Alex Vesia, Brusdar Graterol, Blake Treinen, Corey Knebel and Kenley Jansen combined to allow just three hits the rest of the way.

Phillips struck out three in 1 1/3 innings and was credited with the win.

Atlanta's Eddie Rosario, who homered twice in his second four-hit game of the NLCS in Game 4, went 2 for 4 with a strikeout.

Pitching in his hometown, Fried gave up five runs and eight hits in 4 2/3 innings. The left-hander struck out three and walked two.

"I wasn't executing on the corners like I normally do and when you leave the balls over the middle, normally damage happens," Fried said.

In the feast-or-famine nature of the Dodgers' offense, Cody Bellinger went 3 for 4 with a strikeout and NL batting champion Trea Turner was 3 for 4 with an RBI single in a four-run eighth capped by Pollock's three-run homer.

Chris Taylor of the Dodgers hits a two-run home run in the second inning of Game 5 of the NLCS —the first of three home runs for Taylor in the Los Angeles rout of Atlanta.

Brave New World (Series)

Rosario's heroics land Atlanta in a place that at one time seemed like a second home: The Fall Classic

Braves 4
Dodgers 2

Braves win
series, 4-1

October 23, 2021

ATLANTA — Led by an unlikely hero, the Atlanta Braves are heading back to a place that used to be so familiar to them.

The World Series.

Eddie Rosario capped a remarkable NL Championship Series with a three-run homer, sending the Braves to the biggest stage of all with a 4-2 victory over the defending champion Los Angeles Dodgers on Saturday night.

The Braves won the best-of-seven playoff four games to two, exorcising the demons of last year's NLCS — when Atlanta squandered 2-0 and 3-1 leads against the Dodgers — and advancing to face the AL champion Astros.

Game 1 is Tuesday night at Minute Maid Park in Houston.

"It's a great moment in my life," Rosario said through an interpreter. "But I want more. I want to win the World Series."

The Braves were Series regulars in the 1990s, winning it all in '95 with a team that included Hall of Famers Greg Maddux, Tom Glavine, John Smoltz and Chipper Jones.

That remains their only title in Atlanta. The Braves lost the Series four other times during that decade, a run of postseason disappointment that marred a momentous streak that grew to 14 straight division titles.

After getting swept in the 1999 World Series by the Yankees, the Braves couldn't even get that far in the postseason.

Twenty-two years of frustration, 12 playoff appearances that fell short of a pennant.

Finally, it's over.

"We actually did it," said longtime first baseman Freddie Freeman, sounding a bit bewildered.

Rosario was acquired in a flurry of deals just before the July 30 trade deadline that rebuilt the Braves' depleted outfield, which lost Ronald Acuña Jr. to a season-ending knee injury and slugger Marcell Ozuna to a hand injury and legal troubles.

They weren't missed at all in the NLCS.

"Anything that was thrown at us," Freeman said, "we were able to overcome it."

Rosario set an Atlanta record and became only the fifth player in baseball history to get 14 hits in a postseason series. He was an easy choice as MVP of the series.

Spurred on by chants of "Eddie! Eddie! Eddie" from the raucous sellout crowd of more than 43,000, Rosario finished 14 of 25 (.560) against the Dodgers, with three homers and nine RBIs.

"We just couldn't figure him out," Los Angeles manager Dave Roberts said.

Will Smith worked a perfect ninth for his fourth save of the postseason after a brilliant relief stint by winner Tyler Matzek

Rosario's final hit was certainly the biggest of the 30-year-old Puerto Rican's career.

With the score tied at 1 in the bottom of the fourth, Rosario came up after pinch-hitter Ehire Adrianza extended the inning with a two-out double into the right-field corner. Slow-running catcher Travis d'Arnaud was held at third by coach Ron Washington, surely aware of who was up next.

Rosario got into an extended duel with Walker Buehler, who stepped up to start on three days' rest after ace Max Scherzer wasn't able to go because of a tired arm.

Rosario swung and missed the first two pitches. Then he fouled one off. Then he took a ball. Then he fouled off two more pitches.

Finally, he got one he liked from the Dodgers' 16-game winner — a cutter that Rosario turned into a 105 mph rocket down the right-field line, higher and higher, straight as an arrow until it landed well back into the seats below the Chop House restaurant.

"We got him 0-2 and just couldn't put him away," Roberts said.

Rosario knew it was gone, dancing down the line after delivering a 361-foot finishing shot to a highly paid team that won 106 games during the regular season.

Series MVP Eddie Rosario of the Braves celebrates after Atlanta clinched its first World Series appearance since 1999.

Jorge Solar dives into second ahead of the throw to Los Angeles second baseman Trea Turner for a double during the eighth inning of Game 6 of the NLCS.

Eddie Rosario is congratulated by his Atlanta Braves teammates after hitting a three-run home run in the fourth inning of Game 6.

Eddie Rosario and teammates celebrate a 4-2 series win over the Dodgers in the NLCS at Truist Park.

Trade Wins Pay Dividends

July acquisitions by GM Alex Anthopoulos pave way to World Series

Atlanta had just stumbled again, losing its seventh straight attempt to reach .500.

"This isn't going to define our season, this series," Braves manager Brian Snitker said that night at Citi Field in New York.

Little did he know.

Two days later, general manager Alex Anthopoulos obtained outfielders Eddie Rosario, Adam Duvall and Jorge Soler along with reliever Richard Rodríguez in four swaps in the hours before the July 30 trade deadline, adding to the acquisition of outfielder Joc Pederson two weeks earlier.

"If you go get three and then one of those guys gets hurt, you're in the same boat and then you have the months of August and September and can't go get anybody else," Anthopoulos said. "So let's try to get four and if anything, your bench will be stronger."

Rosario, Duvall and Pederson combined to drive in 17 of Atlanta's 28 runs in its six-game NL Championship Series win over the defending champion Los Angeles Dodgers. Rosario was selected MVP as the Braves advanced to a World Series matchup against the Houston Astros.

Pederson especially has been a pearl of an addition. Even before the Braves tried to earn the team's first World Series championship rings since the Greg Maddux, Tom Glavine, John Smoltz and Chipper Jones club of 1995, he became known for wearing perhaps the most-seen strand of

> **"I think this year has been a testament to how we have handled adversity and how we've turned the page and just kept grinding, kept working."**
>
> Adam Duvall

Alex Anthopoulos, Braves executive vice president and general manager, made savvy trade moves that may have saved the season.

pearls since Jackie O's.

"I just saw the pearls and I was like, you know what? That looks cool," Pederson said. "I've done the black chain and the gold chain and all those different ones and — I think a lot of other players have. But I don't know, kind of caught my eye. I was like, you know, those look good."

Anthopoulos, a 44-year-old Canadian hired as general manager in November 2017 and promoted to president of baseball operations last year, had to remake his outfield in midseason.

Opening day center fielder Cristian Pache injured his right hamstring on May 13 and didn't have another big league at-bat until October. Left fielder Marcell Ozuna broke his left middle and ring fingers with a headfirst slide on May 25, then was arrested four days later on charges of aggravated assault and hasn't returned. Star right fielder Ronald Acuña Jr. tore his right anterior cruciate ligament on July 10, an injury sidelining him until next year.

Many GMs make midseason additions. Seldom do so many jell.

With the deal for Pederson, Anthopoulos sent the clubhouse a message "that we believe in you," recalled star first baseman Freddie Freeman, the reigning NL MVP.

Anthopoulos had gone to his boss, chairman Terry McGuirk, for permission to spend and lifted payroll from $136 million on opening day to $149 million on Aug. 31, still 14th among the 30 teams.

"Terry McGuirk came to me at the All-Star break and said you got whatever you need to go make this club better. Whatever you need. And we went full-speed ahead," Anthopoulous said.

Atlanta lost at Milwaukee hours after the trade deadline, dropping to 51-54. The Braves were third in the NL East, five games back of the New York Mets, one game behind Philadelphia and two games in front of Washington.

"The one thing that's fortunate for us is we're playing in the NL East in 2021," Anthopolous said after the trades. "We're all in it."

Atlanta won five of its next six games to move above .500 for the first time all season on Aug. 8.

Eddie Rosario, right, is congratulated by Joc Pederson after hitting a home run against the Dodgers in the 2021 NLCS.

From left, left fielder Eddie Rosario, center fielder Adam Duvall and right fielder Jorge Soler celebrate against Colorado on Sept. 5.

A Fall Classic Fixture

Charlie Morton lands spot in third World Series in five seasons.

Though the uniform keeps changing, Charlie Morton is becoming a Fall Classic fixture.

Morton is a teammate turned tormentor in Houston, delivering the Astros a 2017 World Series title with a legendary Game 7 performance and denying them a return trip last year as a Tampa Bay Ray. He has slipped quietly back into town, as Morton does, for yet another World Series, this time with the Atlanta Braves.

And that, really, should explain everything: Carrying three franchises into a World Series in a five-year span is legend stuff, a reputation so well-earned that All-Star teammate Freddie Freeman says Morton remains "the best big-game pitcher there is in this sport."

Yet Morton, who has pondered retirement in recent years and turns 38 next month, is far from a mercenary. He leaves behind as much as he brings to the table, striking a balance of reserved and resolute that compels teammates to listen, particularly when he backs up his words with dominance on the mound.

So when Morton takes the ball for Game 1 of this World Series, his presence will extend far beyond the trivia answer as the right-hander who threw the final pitch of a Fall Classic for the Astros, and the first pitch of another against them.

His two seasons here saw him move easily from pitching sage to overall teammate, his accountability extending so far as to express contrition for a sign-stealing scandal that did not directly involve him. They have not forgotten.

"The best you can ever have," says Astros second baseman Jose Altuve. "He's that good. He's amazing."

The recent October resume should be enough, starting with those four innings of two-hit relief to close out the Los Angeles Dodgers in Game 7 of the 2017 World Series, a battle that will be remembered for decades, and for reasons far beyond a clutch relief performance on three days' rest.

Yet the Astros don't have their lone World Series trophy without it.

Morton got the whole face-the-old-team out of the way when he signed a two-year deal with the Tampa Bay Rays and beat them in Game 3 of an AL Division Series that the heavily-favored Astros barely survived in five. In the 2020 playoff bubble, he won ALCS Games 1 and 7 against the Astros, laying the groundwork for a 3-0 Tampa Bay series lead and halting the bleeding when the Astros nearly crawled out of that hole.

You can call it clutch, but current and former teammates see something beyond.

"He's a very special guy, and he's impacted a lot of guys in this clubhouse and a lot of guys who are no longer in this clubhouse," says Astros starter Lance McCullers Jr., who started that 2017 Game 7 but will miss this World Series due to a forearm injury.

"I think what I learned from him the most is just every day at the ballpark is a blessing. Always put your family first and come to the field and be a good teammate and love the guys in the clubhouse and try to be there for guys when you can.

A long-time Astros ace, Charlie Morton cemented his spot as the Braves' top arm, leading them to a World Series berth against his old team.

"Because that's something that Chuck-O was big on."

It is a mentality forged through a 20-year pro career that has moved in anything but a linear fashion, with injuries, maddening inconsistency and a long road to developing an appropriate pitch mix delaying Morton's star appointment. He finally found it as a Philadelphia Phillie in 2016, when he junked a sinkerballer that led to unlucky outcomes and started throwing harder and up in the zone, getting ahead of a trend that would soon consume the industry.

A hamstring injury curtailed that season but the Astros saw enough, gave him a two-year deal and coaxed even more out of him.

When the Rays decided not to pick up a 2021 option, the Braves gave him the same $15 million he earned the previous two seasons. It was a wild full-circle moment for player and the franchise that drafted him in 2002.

"If you have a 14-pronged fork, he's been on every single road," says Freeman, "and it took him a little bit longer than I'm sure he wanted to figure out the success.

"But when he got here, he figured it out."

Long enough to win 107 major league games, make two All-Star teams, win one ring and, Tuesday night in Game 1, shoot for another.

He says he's exchanged recent text messages with Bregman, yet both teams are entering do-not-disturb mode in service of winning a championship. Still, it is October and it is Houston, and the bonds forged and championship won will certainly elicit emotion.

That's just how it goes when you're Morton, who ostensibly leaves it all on the field, yet always has a little bit more to give when he gets back to the clubhouse.

"I'm sure I'm going to feel some things when I get on that mound," says Morton. "I don't think there's any way not to."

Although his 2021 World Series was cut short due to a Game 1 injury, Charlie Morton still played a major role in the Braves' championship.

All In The Family

Father and son to square off in the World Series.

No matter how this year's World Series ends, a Snitker will get a championship ring.

This edition of the Fall Classic is a family affair with Atlanta Braves manager Brian Snitker in the dugout opposite his son, Houston Astros co-hitting coach Troy Snitker.

Close their whole lives, they'll be rivals when the teams take the field for Game 1.

"Quite honestly, tomorrow at 7:09 gametime, he's going to want to kick my (butt)," dad said.

But on the eve of the game, the elder Snitker still found time to play the role of proud papa when talking about his son's success.

"I kind of validated the fact that maybe I did something right, the way he turned out," he said. "He's a heck of a young man."

Troy Snitker grew up in clubhouses and dugouts, following his father as he toiled as a minor league skipper for most of his childhood. Brian Snitker taught his son so much during that time, but as he watched him bounce around teams from Macon, Georgia, to Myrtle Beach, South Carolina, it was not what he said, but what he did that served as the most important lesson.

"Just his work ethic," the 32-year-old Snitker said. "I think that's the biggest thing that I've taken away from him, being able to watch him from a young age at the ballpark. He's so consistent, hard working. He's the same guy every day when you're in the clubhouse with him."

The 66-year-old Snitker spent 15 seasons a manager for various Braves' farm teams before working as Atlanta's third base coach from 2007-2013. He was the manager of the Triple-A Gwinnett Braves from 2013 until becoming the big-league club's interim manager when Fredi González was fired in May 2016.

Brian got the job full-time in 2017 and has led the Braves to the postseason in each of the last four seasons.

"He's just, he's been through so much in his career where there were plenty of times where he could have easily decided to go do something else," his son said. "But he stuck with it."

Troy Snitker coached in college for a bit before joining the Double-A Corpus Christi Hooks as their hitting coach in 2018. He spent just one season there before moving on to work for Houston's major league club.

Brian Snitker is impressed with the way his son has incorporated the things he learned about baseball growing up with his dad with the newer side of the sport.

"I love the fact that he's meshed (things)," Brian Snitker said. "Because I raised him in a dugout, on a bus, on the field a long, a long time ago before analytics were ever invented. I think he's a good blend of the old-school way of doing things and he's very open and gets all the new information that's out there. I think it's a good mix."

The entire family is, of course, thrilled about two Snitkers being in the World Series. But for Ronnie Snitker, wife of Brian Snitker and Troy Snitker's mom, navigating through this week might be a bit difficult.

No telling yet what she'll wear, how she'll represent her family's teams.

"I think she's just slightly overwhelmed at the moment trying to get her mind around the concept that this is actually happening," Troy Snitker said.

And after the Snitker men finishing raving about each other, they both agreed that the true star of this week is Ronnie.

"If it wasn't for her, he or I wouldn't be here honestly," her husband said. "She's allowed Troy and myself to follow our dream, and we're very appreciative."

Houston Astros hitting coach Troy Snitker, left, stands with his father, Braves manager Brian Snitker, during 2019 Spring Training.

Freddie's Time

Freeman finally gets his chance on the big stage of the World Series.

When people in baseball talk about "Freddie," no one wonders whom they're referring to. Few players are as identifiable by their first name as Freddie Freeman.

He is the Atlanta Braves' friendly first baseman next door who greets all arrivals with a joke or a smile, the rare star who is so entrenched with his franchise that it is almost impossible to picture him in any other uniform.

He is familiar, forthcoming and fearlessly self-deprecating, the kind of guy who doesn't seem to have an intimidating bone in his body — until he steps into the batter's box. That may be the only place where friendly Freddie Freeman inspires abject fear, and the Houston Astros must be ready when they host Game 1 of the World Series.

But on June 4, steady Freddie Freeman was frustrated. In fact, he was fuming. He was hitting .226. Everything he hit hard seemed to find a glove.

Everyone tried to reassure him, but he couldn't really hear them. After one particularly frustrating game, Freeman spoke with his father, who recited numbers such as exit velocity and expected batting average to try to convince his son that the skid couldn't last forever.

"He was trying to give me all the numbers to make me feel better, being a dad," Freeman said then. "I'm just staring at him on the FaceTime, fuming through the phone because I don't want to hear that."

What he wanted was to see a three at the front of his batting average. But day by day, .300 seemed further and further from the realm of possibility. At times, even .250 seemed out of reach.

His Braves were watching their chances slip, too. Ace Mike Soroka had yet to pitch and ended up being out for the year. Catcher Travis d'Arnaud was in a multi-month injury absence. Ronald Acuña Jr. was having an MVP season that would soon end with a heartbreaking torn ACL. That this would be the year the Braves would break through ... well, unlikely was an understatement.

By the last day of the regular season, Freeman was hitting .300 on the dot, and his Braves were National League East champions.

"Every single year you come into spring training expecting to get to the World Series. That's been my goal every single year," Freeman said. "You never self-doubt. You just see what this team has done the last four years, and you could see what was coming through those rebuild years, too, and you just get excited."

Maybe Freeman always believed, but he certainly wasn't happy during his skid. Teammates and coaches praise him as much for his talent as for his demeanor. They say he is as consistent as they come, as unwilling to let success change his approach as he is to let failure influence it. But in that early June stretch when nothing was working, even Freeman couldn't hide his frustration.

"What did everyone else say?" shortstop Dansby Swanson replied when asked what he saw from Freeman during those frustrating weeks, as if gauging how honest he should be.

"He was miserable," Swanson offered.

"It wasn't like a week. It wasn't like a 'that's baseball' thing," he added. "We were just bad. He wasn't great, either, and it wears on you. And it wore on him."

Hitting coach Kevin Seitzer said he told Freeman what everyone else was telling him. He looked at his batting average on balls in play (.222 as of June 4), saw his strikeouts weren't climbing, noticed the walk numbers were right where they would normally be.

Freddie Freeman watches the ball off of his bat during a game against the Brewers in the 2021 NLDS.

"He knows when he's right, and he knows when he's off. And when he's off, well, he's not normal — put it that way," Seitzer said. "But I just told him to stay right where he was at."

Seitzer and Freeman have worked together since the 2015 season, so Seitzer knows exactly what drills to add to Freeman's dogged routine when issues emerge. But Seitzer said that even during his early-season slump, they only turned to those drills two or three times. There was nothing to fix. Freeman just had to wait for the game to reward his talent, as it had for a decade.

That talent, which will be on display on the game's biggest stage for the first time, is almost universally regarded as some of the best baseball has to offer. Max Scherzer called Freeman "the best hitter I've had to face" and once said there were times during his Washington Nationals tenure when he would tell his manager before the seventh or eighth inning that he had enough left for a batter or two — but probably not enough to get Freeman a fourth time.

"Even if you throw a pretty good location, you locate it pretty good, that doesn't matter against him. He can still hit it out of the ballpark."

Max Scherzer

Seitzer called Freeman the best hitter he has ever coached because he can hit almost anything. In 2021, Freeman hit .339 against four-seam fastballs, .319 against sliders, .273 against curveballs and .323 against change-ups. He hit .306 against pitches on the inner third, .319 against pitches in the middle third and .270 against pitches on the outer third.

"Doesn't matter what pitch you throw — if you overexpose any one of your pitches, he can hit it out of the ballpark at will," Scherzer said during the NLCS. "Even if you throw a pretty good location, you locate it pretty good, that doesn't matter against him. He can still hit it out of the ballpark."

Freddie Freeman walks with his child, Charlie Freeman, during a workout ahead of the NLCS against the Dodgers on October 14.

Clutch Performer

Rosario's playoff tear helps Braves see potential for sustained success.

Eddie Rosario talked the other day about his lucky lumber, a 33 1/2-inch, 31-ounce Chandler Bat that started to heat up with a four-hit night in mid-September.

"I've been using that bat that I hit for the cycle with and it has not disappointed," he said through a translator after his second four-hit game of the NL Championship Series. "Man, this bat has not let me down yet."

Well, he topped that on Saturday night, becoming MVP of the NLCS. As the crowd chanted his name, Rosario hoisted the award.

"It's truly a great moment, not just in my career, but in my life, as well," he said. "But I want more. I want to win the World Series."

Rosario hit a tiebreaking, three-run homer off Dodgers ace Walker Buehler in the fourth inning, lifting the Atlanta Braves over Los Angeles 4-2 for their first NL pennant since 1999 and a Series matchup with the Houston Astros.

"We just couldn't figure him out," Dodgers manager Dave Roberts said. "He beat us the other way. He beat us to the pull side. He got hits off lefties, off righties. We tried to spin him. We went hard. We just didn't have an answer for him."

Less than three months after he was traded by Cleveland, which sent the Braves money to take him away, the 30-year-old outfielder had six multi-hit games against the Dodgers. He hit .560 (14 for 25) with three homers and nine RBIs, giving him a 1.040 slugging percentage and 1.647 OPS.

He has hit safely in all 10 postseason games, batting .474 with 11 RBIs from the leadoff spot, ahead of Freddie Freeman.

"It doesn't matter what arm they're throwing with, he's just so locked in," Braves manager Brian Snitker said. "I don't know that I've ever seen a guy like that for this long while now."

No hit was bigger than Rosario's home run in the fourth inning. With the score 1-1, he fouled off three pitches around a ball that left the count at 1-2, then sent a cutter down the right-field line at 105 mph, the ball carrying 361 feet.

With 14 hits, he tied the record for a postseason series, a mark he shares with Albert Pujols and Hideki Matsui (2004), Kevin Youkilis (2007) and Marco Scutaro (2012).

"I feel like I've had a good first half of my career," Rosario said. "I feel like I was vying for two All-Star appearances. I feel like I deserved them. That didn't happen, so I kept just vying for the next award or accolade, and this was it."

Before this October, Rosario was known mostly for stepping up against Cleveland. During six seasons with Minnesota, he hit .301 with 22 homers and 47 RBIs in 93 games against the Indians, prompting Cleveland to sign him as a free agent to an $8 million, one-year contract with funds saved after trading Francisco Lindor and Carlos Carrasco to the New York Mets.

Eddie Rosario swings for a two-run triple against San Francisco on August 29.

Rosario batted .254 with seven homers and 46 RBIs for the Indians and was on the injured list with an oblique strain when he was traded to Atlanta on July 30 for infielder Pablo Sandoval, who was immediately released. Cleveland sent the Braves $500,000 to offset part of the $2,795,699 remaining in Rosario's salary.

"I wanted to illustrate the type of ballplayer that I am and showcase that I am capable of doing these things," Rosario said.

He didn't return the major leagues until Aug. 28, and he hit .271 with seven homers and 16 RBIs in 96 at-bats for the Braves, one of four outfielders brought in along with Joc Pederson, Adam Duvall and Jorge Soler.

> **"It motivates me to come through in big moments."**
>
> Eddie Rosario

"To be honest, it was a competition at first," Rosario said. "All four of us showed up and I think we all wanted to get some playing time and be in the lineup. So for me it was definitely a little bit of a sense of urgency to kind of push the envelope a little bit and try to work my way into the lineup."

Turns out, heat helped Rosario's bat to get hot.

"The first two months is 40 degrees all the time in Cleveland," said Rosario, who hails from Puerto Rico. "When it's hot I feel better."

Rosario hit for the cycle on Sept. 19 against San Francisco, helping the Braves stop a four-game skid and build a two-game lead over Philadelphia in the NL East.

He batted .308 (4 for 13) with two RBIs in the four-game Division Series win over Milwaukee.

Heading into the Series, fans chanting "Ed-die! Ed-die!" have become a nightly occurrence at Truist Park.

"It motivates me to come through in big moments," Rosario said. "The pitcher hears a little bit and it almost forces him to throw the pitch you want to see."

Eddie Rosario kisses the NLCS Most Valuable Player trophy after the Braves' six-game series win over the Dodgers to seal the NL pennant.

Eddie Rosario said hearing fans cheer for him gets in the head of opponents: "The pitcher hears a little bit and it almost forces him to throw the pitch you want to see."

Soler Power

Leadoff homer lifts Braves to early edge in series despite loss of Charlie Morton.

Braves 6
Astros 2

Braves lead series, 1-0.

October 26, 2021

HOUSTON — A healthy swing by Jorge Soler powered the Atlanta Braves to a smashing start in the World Series.

In the lineup for the first time since a positive COVID-19 test, Soler became the first player to begin a World Series with a home run and the Braves, despite the loss of pitcher Charlie Morton to a broken leg, hushed the Houston Astros 6-2 in Game 1.

Boosted by a strong bullpen effort, Adam Duvall's two-run homer and a late sacrifice fly from Freddie Freeman, the Braves coasted in their first Series appearance since Chipper Jones and their Big Three aces ascended in 1999.

"So much happened really quick," Atlanta manager Brian Snitker said.

Every Braves starter wound up getting a hit and more than four hours later, this was the scene in their dugout: outlandish outfielder Joc Pederson sipping a glass of red wine and smoking cigars with closer Will Smith.

That victory party lasted a couple of minutes until a security guard ambled over and told them it was a smoke-free building.

Jose Altuve, Carlos Correa and the Astros, meanwhile, mostly looked lost at the plate. This is their third World Series in five seasons — and first since their 2017 illegal sign-stealing scheme was revealed.

"You've just got to like blow this game off and then come back and realize that tomorrow's — that's the beauty of baseball," 72-year-old Astros manager Dusty Baker said. "Tomorrow's another day, and who knows? That's the way I look at it."

Soler's no-doubt jolt into the left-field seats on Framber Valdez's third pitch quickly drained all the juice out of Minute Maid Park, quieting a sellout crowd.

"The energy was amazing and electric, especially after we took a 1-0 lead after that home run," Soler said through a translator.

As for his feat?

"I didn't know that was a thing until I was told a little later on in the game," he said.

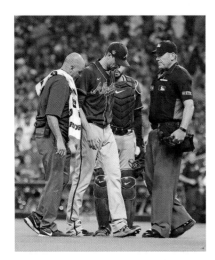

Above: Braves starter Charlie Morton leaves in the fourth inning of Game 1 with a broken leg.

Right: Jorge Soler connects on a solo home run on the first at-bat of the game against the Astros.

Moments later, Ozzie Albies stole a base and Austin Riley hit an RBI double, taking a rare swing at a 3-0 pitch.

Soler, who missed five playoff games after testing positive for the coronavirus, added an RBI grounder in the second. And when Duvall launched a two-run homer, it was 5-0 and the Braves had made even more October history — the only team to score in each of the first three innings in a World Series opener.

"I think we obviously swung the bats there early pretty well, and doing that on the road, kind of getting them first at-bat jitters out of the way, it's big," Duvall said.

At that point, Braves batters were far from the only ones making noise. The few Atlanta fans sprinkled in the sea of orange had started their familiar chop chant, too.

Baseball can be a fickle game, and the fates can spin faster than the best curveball. Because in the bottom of the third, Atlanta absorbed its own big hit.

As he struck out Altuve, Morton suddenly grimaced and took an awkward step. His teammates, Snitker and a trainer soon joined him on the mound, and just like that, Morton was gone. Turned out a hard comebacker by Yuli Gurriel that ricocheted off Morton's leg to Freeman at first base for an out to begin the second had done more damage than anyone realized.

Morton stayed in for another inning, amazingly, before gingerly walking off with a fractured right fibula. The 37-year-old righty, the winning pitcher for the Astros in Game 7 of the 2017 World Series, will be replaced on the roster. He's expected to be OK for spring training.

"God bless him, I hate it for him. Really hate it for him," Snitker said.

Atlanta's Jorge Soler celebrates his home run with Freddie Freeman during the first inning of Game 1.

The Braves' Dansby Swanson scores past Houston catcher Jason Castro on a sacrifice fly during the eighth inning of Game 1.

The Braves stand on the field at Minute Maid Park in Houston ahead of their first World Series game since 1999.

Unsettled, and All Square

Astros tee
off in second
inning, halt
Braves'
postseason
momentum.

Astros 7
Braves 2

Series
tied, 1-1.

October 27, 2021

Houston — Max Fried was pitching like the lefty ace he has been most of this season for the Atlanta Braves, retiring 10 batters in a row in his first World Series start.

The only problem was that it came after a horrendous four-run second inning that put the Houston Astros ahead to stay, and sent Fried to his second consecutive loss at a time when the Braves really need him the most.

Overall, it was another postseason dud for Fried.

"Obviously, I'm not happy about it. Playoffs is a big momentum game," Fried said. "You've got to do everything you can to keep the crooked number off the scoreboard."

With a chance to send Atlanta home with a 2-0 lead in its first World Series since 1999, Fried instead allowed six runs and seven hits while pitching into the sixth inning of a 7-2 loss. He did strike out six with only one walk.

It came six days after Fried gave up five runs and eight hits over 4 2/3 innings in a potential NL Championship Series clincher in Game 5. That instead became an 11-2 loss to the Los Angeles Dodgers and pushed back another two days the Braves clinching the National League pennant.

That was the first time since June 1 that Fried didn't make it past the fifth inning. Now he has losing decisions in consecutive games for only the second time all year — he lost his final two starts in July before a dominating finish to the regular season, and a solid start to these playoffs.

The Braves had won 6-2 in Game 1, getting 6 2/3 solid innings from their bullpen after starter Charlie Morton was struck by a comebacker and suffered a broken right fibula. Morton is done for the series.

"That's terrific for him to be able to get into the sixth there, especially after they were able to score the runs they did," catcher Travis d'Arnaud said of Fried. "It gave our bullpen the rest they needed after yesterday with the bullpen game."

Manager Brian Snitker said he was still having a hard time convincing himself that Fried actually struggled.

"The first inning, they did some really good hitting. The second inning, when they scored, it was kind of a weird inning, you know what I mean," Snitker said. "It wasn't like he was getting banged around. Balls that found holes, checked swings, we threw a ball away. It was just a weird inning. But I thought his stuff was really good."

Astros leadoff hitter Jose Altuve, scuffling with a .178 average this October and coming off his first three-strikeout postseason game in Game 1, started things off against Fried when he scorched a double into the left field corner.

"You can be 0 for 20, but what about if you get the big hit? So that's what playoffs is about," Altuve said. "I don't care if I went 0 for 5 last night."

Michael Brantley hit a flyball that sent Altuve to third before Alex Bregman scored him with a sacrifice fly.

After d'Arnaud homered on a full-count pitch with two outs in the second to tie the game, Carlos Correa struck out leading off the bottom of the inning. But the last four hitters in Houston's lineup then had consecutive singles — and all of them scored, with help from a throwing error by left fielder Eddie Rosario and a wild pitch by Fried.

Kyle Tucker, Yuli Gurriel, rookie José Siri and Martin Maldonado had the four consecutive singles. Siri drove in the first run with an infield hit and Maldonado got an RBI on his hit to left, with Siri then scoring the second run after Rosario threw toward an unoccupied third base for an error. Fried then had a wild pitch before Brantley's sharp RBI single.

Fried finally got out of the inning on Bregman's grounder to third, and the pitcher didn't allow another runner until walking Yordan Alvarez leading off the sixth. The Braves starter was then gone after Correa singled.

Atlanta's Joc
Pederson argues a
call with home plate
umpire Ron Kulpa
during the eighth
inning of a frustrating
Game 2 loss in
Houston.

Masterclass on the Mound

Anderson throws five no-hit innings, bullpen completes the shutout.

Braves 2
Astros 0

Braves lead series, 2-1.

October 29, 2021

ATLANTA — Ian Anderson had pitched five no-hit innings when Brian Snitker walked up to the 23-year-old and said, "That's it."

"Are you sure? Are you sure?" the rookie right-hander asked.

"I'm going with my gut right here," the manager said.

On a night that showed how much baseball has evolved in the Analytics Age, Anderson and the Braves' bullpen took a no-hit bid into the eighth inning, Austin Riley and Travis d'Arnaud drove in runs and Atlanta beat the Houston Astros 2-0 to grab a 2-1 World Series lead.

Pinch-hitter Aledmys Díaz blooped a single leading off the eighth against Tyler Matzek that dropped in front of Eddie Rosario, just 232 feet from home plate, for Houston's first hit as the left fielder pulled up to avoid colliding with shortstop Dansby Swanson.

Alex Bregman grounded a single through the wide-open right side of a shifted infield leading off the ninth against Will Smith, who remained perfect in five save chances this postseason.

Anderson threw 76 pitches, and A.J. Minter, Luke Jackson, Matzek and Smith combined for the last 57 of the 18th two-hit shutout in Series history.

"Obviously you want the chance to compete, especially on the biggest stage like this is," Anderson said. "But, yeah, I knew he wasn't going to budge."

Snitker didn't consider giving Anderson a chance to join the Yankees' Don Larsen, whose perfect game in 1956 is the only Series no-hitter.

"He wasn't going to pitch a nine-inning no-hitter," Snitker said. "He wasn't going to have pitches to do that."

Anderson struck out four and walked three, throwing just 39 of 76 pitches for strikes.

"He was effectively wild," Astros manager Dusty Baker said. "Our guys never could zero in on the strikes."

Anderson is 4-0 in his postseason career with a 1.26 ERA.

"He's turned into an absolute animal, a beast in the playoffs," Matzek said.

"Luke Jackson didn't know. Minter didn't know," Matzek said of the no-hit bid. "After I got done with my inning, they went up and said: `Hey, did you know you gave up the first hit?' And I said, `Yeah, I did know. I paid attention.'"

Of the 60 previous times the Series was tied 1-1, the Game 3 winner went on to win 39 times — including six of the last nine.

Riley hit an RBI double in the third on a cutter from rookie Luis Garcia after Freddie Freeman singled, and d'Arnaud added his second Series homer in the eighth, a 437-foot drive off Kendall Graveman that was d'Arnaud's first long ball at home since September 2020.

Atlanta, which stranded nine runners, improved to 6-0 this postseason at Truist Park, which opened in 2017 and where it has won 11 of its last 12 games. The Braves stopped a five-game home World Series losing streak.

Houston, the top-hitting team in the majors during the season with a .267 average, was limited to seven baserunners.

"We didn't swing it for one game," Bregman said. "I think we flush it and move on to the next day and have a short memory."

Díaz's hit ended the longest no-hit bid in the Series since Game 2 in 1967. Pinch-runner Jose Siri stole second with two outs in the eighth and went to third when d'Arnaud's throw skipped into center field for an error, but Siri was stranded when Michael Brantley popped out against Matzek.

Snitker, in his 44th season with the Braves, knows a few years ago he would have let Anderson stay in.

"The me of old, probably a couple years ago," Snitker said, "I'm like how the hell am I doing this?

Ian Anderson delivers in Game 3 against the Astros. Anderson pitched five no-hit innings to wrest control of the World Series back from Houston.

The Braves celebrate at Truist Park after taking a 2-1 World Series lead.

Atlanta's Travis d'Arnaud connects on a home run during the eighth inning in Game 3 against Houston.

On the Edge of History

Braves grit, grind and finally rally for a 3-2 win to come within a game of a championship.

Braves 3
Astros 2

Braves lead series, 3-1.

October 30, 2021

ATLANTA — This Atlanta Braves team couldn't have picked a more fitting way to move to the brink of a World Series championship.

A pitcher who spent most of the year in the minors kept them in it.

A slugger who came in a flurry of trades won it for them.

If this gritty bunch can do it one more time, the Braves will have their first Series title in 26 years.

Dansby Swanson and pinch-hitter Jorge Soler connected for back-to-back homers in the seventh inning, propelling the Braves to a 3-2 victory over the Houston Astros and a commanding 3-1 Series lead.

Game 5 is Sunday night. The Braves can wrap up the championship on their home field, just as they did two stadiums ago when they beat the Cleveland Indians in 1995.

They've sure been tough at home, improving to 7-0 this postseason.

"It's just such a cool moment for this city," Swanson said. "But we've got one more. They've got a great ballclub over there and we can't take anything for granted."

That triumph more than a quarter-century ago at the old Atlanta-Fulton County Stadium remains the franchise's only World Series crown since moving to the Deep South in 1966.

This is the closest the Braves have been to a second title since then.

What an improbable crown it would be.

With former president Donald Trump watching from a private box down the right-field line, the Braves got a huge boost from a most unlikely player.

Former first-round draft pick Kyle Wright, who made only two appearances in the majors during a season spent mostly at Triple-A Gwinnett, got through 4 2/3 critical innings out of the bullpen after surprise starter Dylan Lee retired only one hitter.

Wright was hardly overpowering, giving up five hits — including a solo homer by Jose Altuve in the fourth that staked the Astros to a 2-0 lead — and three walks. But he continually pitched out of trouble, giving the Braves a semblance of hope until the offense woke up.

"He probably doesn't realize what he did, how big it was," Atlanta manager Brian Snitker said. "I'm so proud how he handled the situation."

Wright has a career record of 2-8 with a 6.56 ERA. In two 2021 starts for the Braves, he was 0-1 with a 9.95 ERA.

"Honestly, I was a little lost," he conceded.

In the sixth, Eddie Rosario became the first Atlanta hitter to get past first base with a one-out double off Brooks Raley.

Rosario wound up scoring on another clutch postseason hit by Austin Riley, who lined a two-out single to left against Phil Maton.

The Braves left the bases loaded, but they weren't done. Just like that, they stunningly engineered the first lead change of the entire Series, with Swanson and Soler becoming the third duo in World Series history to hit back-to-back homers that tied and put a team ahead.

The first two guys to do it were named Babe Ruth and Lou Gehrig.

Facing Cristian Javier, Swanson went the opposite way for a homer that tied the game at 2, the ball hit so hard that it ricocheted off the tabled section in the right-field stands and rolled all the way back to the infield.

"It was like, 'You know what? Let's get rid of everything else and just compete,'" Swanson said. "And you know what? Something amazing happened."

The celebration had barely simmered down when Soler, one of four outfielders acquired in trades by general manager Alex Anthopoulos, stepped to the plate as a pinch-hitter.

On a 2-1 pitch from Javier, Soler put a charge into a hanging slider and drove it into the Astros' bullpen in left. Yordan Alvarez was left hanging helplessly atop the short fence as the ball sailed over his head.

The Braves' Jorge Soler hits a home run during the seventh inning in Game 4, the second of back-to-back home runs in the crucial inning for Atlanta.

Dansby Swanson connects on his solo home run in the seventh inning of Game 4 against the Astros.

Braves left fielder Eddie Rosario stretches to catch a fly ball hit by the Astros' Jose Altuve during the eighth inning of Game 4 of the World Series.

Back to Houston

Astros mount
furious rally
after early
Braves grand
slam to extend
series.

Astros 9
Braves 5

Braves lead
series, 3-2.

October 31, 2021

ATLANTA — Just in time, Carlos Correa and the Houston Astros broke out the bats.

Because if they had waited any longer, this World Series would've been over.

Staggered by Adam Duvall's grand slam in the first inning, Correa and Alex Bregman ended their slumps in a hurry. They kept swinging, too, refusing to let their season slip away and rallying past the Atlanta Braves 9-5 to cut their Series deficit to 3-2.

The Braves might not admit it was a deflating defeat; 66-year-old manager Brian Snitker is too steady and savvy for that. But by any measure in the Analytics Age, this had to sting.

"I'm just glad we get to go back to Houston. That was our goal today," Astros skipper Dusty Baker said.

Correa came through with three hits after getting moved up to third in the lineup for Game 5 while Bregman was dropped to seventh. Martín Maldonado found three different ways to drive in runs and pinch-hitter Marwin Gonzalez blooped a two-out, two-run single in the fifth for a 7-5 lead.

A matchup of bullpens turned into the first high-scoring game of this Fall Classic, and the highest-scoring team in the majors this year won it.

"We've got a clubhouse full of bad dudes in there. And our lineup is very deep," Correa said.

The star shortstop doubled and singled twice, driving in two runs. His RBI single in the eighth padded the lead and as Jose Altuve got congrats in the dugout after scoring, the Fox TV mics picked up someone on the bench yelling "It's time!"

"Before the game we talked and we said, 'We're not gonna give up,'" Correa said. "We're gonna go out there fighting."

Atlanta had been 7-0 at home in the postseason, and a boisterous crowd inside Truist Park and packed plaza outside came early hoping to celebrate its first championship since 1995.

"If we win the World Series, it doesn't matter where it is," Snitker said. "I'd have loved to have done it in front of our fans. Hopefully, we can do it the next couple of days."

Duvall's slam sent a dozen Braves careening from the dugout, a full-out frenzy of hollering, twirling and dancing.

"We celebrated it. We got excited, and that's what you do when you hit home runs — but it's a long game. That happened in the bottom of the first. It's a nine-inning game, and they didn't quit," Duvall said.

Indeed, any victory party was premature — even after Freddie Freeman's long homer put Atlanta ahead 5-4.

Instead, the Astros hushed those fans and the Braves, pulling off a big comeback.

Down 4-0 after Duvall tagged Framber Valdez, the Astros began to chip away against surprise starter Tucker Davidson.

Bregman got things going with an RBI double that ended the Astros' rut with runners in scoring position and Maldonado — 4 for 41 in the postseason at that point — followed with a sacrifice fly that pulled them to 4-2.

An error by shortstop Dansby Swanson helped Houston tie it in the third. Altuve reached on the misplay and Michael Brantley walked, ending Davidson's day. Correa greeted reliever Jesse Chavez with an RBI double, and a run-scoring grounder by Yuli Gurriel made it 4-all.

Freeman untied it moments later, connecting for a 460-foot home run that matched the longest of his career.

But having finally gotten loose at the plate, the Astros weren't going quietly.

Singles by Correa and Gurriel and a two-out intentional walk to Bregman loaded the bases in the fifth. Lefty reliever A.J. Minter lost Maldonado for a walk that tied it, and Gonzalez singled for the lead.

Braves pitcher Drew Smyly leaves the field during the ninth inning in Game 5 after Atlanta fell, 9-5, and sent the series back to Houston.

World Champions!

Series MVP Jorge Soler sets tone with mammoth homer, Braves bring home first championship since 1995.

Braves 7
Astros 0

Braves win series, 4-2

November 2, 2021

HOUSTON — They were counted out by everyone, but the only the ones who actually counted, refused to believe it.

Too many injuries. Too many slumps.

Atlanta blocked out the noise, and Tuesday night at Minute Maid Park were dancing and celebrating, standing alone atop the baseball world.

Atlanta is the World Series champions, routing the Houston Astros, 7-0, to win the series, 4 games to 2, for its first championship since 1995.

Atlanta's latest heroes were outfielder Jorge Soler and ace Max Fried. Soler, who opened the postseason testing positive for COVID-19, hit his third homer of the World Series, a mammoth 3-run shot in the third inning. Fried, who had badly struggled in his last two postseason starts, made it all stand up with six dominant shutout innings.

The truth is that this was a team full of heroes night after night.

Despite losing their best hitter (Ronald Acuna), their best slugger (Marcel Ozuna), and one of their best starters (Mike Soroka), Atlanta simply refused to quit.

GM Alex Anthopoulos, believing in their team's heart and pride, pulled off six trades, including four outfielders, while 66-year-old manager Brian Snitker pulled out all of the stops.

They were 52-54 at the July 30 trade deadline. They weren't above .500 until Aug. 6.

This team simply could not be measured by any computer, logarithms or spreadsheets.

"That's something analytics never can have a hand in," said Atlanta closer Will Smith, "is chemistry and getting along with each other. We legitimately love each other in that clubhouse. We say it out loud."

Who would have realized the catalyst of their attack would be Soler, acquired in the final hours of the trade deadline from the Kansas City Royals? He singlehandedly out-homered the Astros in the Series, 3-2, but none were bigger than his third-hitting blast.

Soler got ahead 3-1 in the count when Astros rookie starter Luis Garcia, pitching on three days' rest, couldn't throw his cutter for a strike.

He took an 81-mph slider for strike 2, and then hit two hard fouls on an 80-mph slider and a 96-mph fastball.

Garcia came back with an 83-mph cutter.

Soler hit it out of the building.

The homer was officially measured at 446 feet, clocked at 109.6-mph off his bat, but it looked more like 546 feet.

It was all that Fried needed, pitching like the guy who dominated the National League the second half instead of the one battered for a 10.24 ERA in his last two postseason starts.

Fried absolutely suffocated the Astros' lineup. He gave up just four hits and no walks in six innings, without permitting a baserunner to reach second base after the first inning.

Yet, for a scary moment, it looked like Fried might not even get out of the first inning.

He gave up an infield single to leadoff hitter Jose Altuve, and then Michael Brantley hit a slow roller to the right of first baseman Freddie Freeman. Freeman picked it up, but Fried was late covering. When Fried caught the ball, he missed the bag, and Brantley's left foot came down hard on Fried's right ankle, spiking him.

The Atlanta trainers rushed to the mound, making sure that Fried was ok, and who would ever have known it would turn out to be the best thing to happen to him.

Fried, facing the heart of the order with two runners on, no outs and a screaming sellout crowd, exhaled, and calmly struck Carlos Correa, induced a soft groundout by Yordan Alvarez, and struck out Yuli Gurriel.

Threat over. Inning over. And for all practical purposes, game over.

Fried never permitted the Astros to even think about getting their offense started, while Atlanta kept pouring it on with homers by Dansby Swanson and Freeman.

"I think as a kid you look forward to winning the World Series and contributing in any way," Fried said. "To be able to be here in this moment, I'm just extremely thankful."

The Atlanta Braves celebrate the final out of Game 6, completing a 7-0 victory to bring the first World Series championship to Atlanta since 1995.

World Series MVP Jorge Soler connects a three-run home run during the third inning of Game 6, the first runs of the game.

Braves designated hitter Jorge Soler, who hit three home runs during the series, holds up the World Series MVP trophy.

WILLIE MAYS
WORLD ⚾ SERIES
MOST VALUABLE PLAYER
2021
PRESENTED BY 🔶 CHEVROLET

Braves first baseman Freddie Freeman celebrates after making the final out of Atlanta's World Series victory.